BOSCH

MARIO BUSSAGLI

GROSSET & DUNLAP
Publishers - New York

First American edition published 1967 by Grosset & Dunlap, Inc.
All rights reserved
Translated from the Italian by Claire Pace
Translation copyright © 1967 by Thames and Hudson, London
Copyright © 1966 by Sadea Editore, Firenze
Library of Congress Catalog Card Number: 67-24230

Printed and bound in Italy

Life

If we knew more details about the life of Jeroen Anthoniszoon van Aken – better known under the pseudonym
(invented by himself) of 'Hieronymus Bosch', with which
he signed his paintings – many intriguing facets of his
enigmatic art would become much clearer. The ambiguous,
baffling symbols which abound in his work – springing
from a boundless power of fantasy and used with a very
definite purpose – would take on a more precise meaning.
Perhaps they might lose that aura of mystery which now
surrounds them; but the aesthetic value of his work would
be more genuinely appreciated. For, even now, the complex
personality of this great artist presents us with both a critical
problem and a psychological riddle: was he an anguished
heretic who confessed his disbelief, by implication, in his
art; or an ironically-minded believer, mockingly cynical
about human nature; or a mystic of impregnable faith; or
indeed all these things simultaneously? What *is* certain is that
the paintings themselves – their symbolism, their visions
of monsters and devils – embody (even for late fifteenth-
century Flanders) an exceptional spiritual experience, the
symptom of a desperate desire to express a 'message',
something new and different which is difficult to reconcile
with the middle-class complacency of the wealthy and
eminent Jeroen van Aken, as he appears from the scanty
evidence at our disposal.

The mystery of Bosch is contained in his work, while even
his surname (which is fairly familiar as that of a family of
good painters) varies between different spellings – appearing
as Aken, Aeken, Aquen, and Acken; this further complicates
the historian's not entirely straightforward task. Born in
about 1450 at 's Hertogenbosch (that is, Bois-le-Duc), a
small town near Antwerp, he derived the pseudonym by
which he became famous from the last syllable of the name
of the town. It is, possibly, a vague allusion to the 'wood'
of contradictions and tormented forces in his own personality; or maybe he simply chose a sound and sense which

imply no more than his fondness for his birthplace. His father, Anthonis van Aken, was a painter, as were his two paternal uncles and also his grandfather, Jan van Aken, who is the best known of the family (after Jeroen) – chiefly for a fresco *Crucifixion* in the city Cathedral, dated 1444.

Nearly all our evidence about Bosch is provided by the documents in the archives of the Lieve-Vrouve Broederschap – that is, the Brotherhood of Our Lady. From these documents, we know that in 1478 he married the 25-year-old Aleid van Meervenne, a wealthy and aristocratic young woman, who brought him a substantial dowry and to whom he owed his slow but sure ascent in the wary society of 's Hertogenbosch. In the same year or the following one his father died; but it was only in 1480-1 that he completed a triptych (commissioned by the Brotherhood) that his father himself had left unfinished. This shows that he was already well known and well thought of. In 1486, thanks to his wife's social standing, he took vows and was raised to the rank of 'sworn brother', thus becoming an eminent citizen. The records of the Brotherhood also state that, between 1493 and 1494, Bosch embarked on, and brought to completion, the drawings which were to decorate the Chapel of the same Brotherhood in the Cathedral of St John. All these drawings, except one, have now been destroyed – as indeed has much of Bosch's work, which has suffered, perhaps more than that of other artists, from the iconoclastic frenzy of the Reformation. The records of the Brotherhood mentioned his death, in 1516 – very briefly, but describing him as '*insignis pictor*' and '*seer vermaerd schilder*' as if to put the seal on the reputation he had already won through a lifetime of astounding, and diverse, activity.

The facts at our disposal, then, are few indeed; such as they are, they reflect a life that was apparently calm, and that was, it seems, centred exclusively on urban society and an upper-middle-class milieu. But appearances may be deceptive here, for the society in which Bosch lived was far more varied and complex than it seems to our eyes today. The small town of 's Hertogenbosch, according to the Italian historian Ludovico Guiccardini, in his *Descrittione di tutti i paesi bassi* (Antwerp 1567) was known for the production of fine cloth, knives, and exquisite brooches; in Bosch's day it was one of the most important cities in Brabant. Though provincial, it was not unaware of cultural and spiritual matters. There was a college of the Brothers of the Common Life, which had been founded by one of the disciples of Jan van Ruysbroeck, Gerhard Groote, towards the end of the fourteenth century; and it was in this college that Erasmus of Rotterdam, when he was very young, spent three years of his life. Undoubtedly, too, the underground heresy of the Adamites must have existed secretly; they believed in universal resurrection and in the Free Spirit. They also believed that sin was the work of God, and therefore refused to consider it as evil. It is even possible that some Adamites and their sympathizers – despite the firm hostility of those who supported the more mystical doctrines propounded by Ruysbroeck – actually belonged to the same Brotherhood which received Bosch.

The invention of printing put into circulation on a scale hitherto unimagined alchemical works of varying levels of profundity; it is, perhaps, not entirely fortuitous that Tondalus's Book of *Visions* was reprinted in this very town of 's Hertogenbosch, in 1484. Moreover, the Brotherhood to which the painter belonged did not confine its functions to prayer, aid, burials, or other works of charity, but also expressed its obligations in productions of a more or less religious nature, in symbolic, moralistic ballets, in fantastic choreography where horrific and demonic themes recurred – in perfect accord with the spirit of the age, half way between licentiousness and heresy. It was these productions which were later to be the object of Erasmus's courteous attack; he subjects them, though indirectly, to ridicule in his *Exorcismus sive spectrum*. It is highly probable that Bosch played no small part in organizing them, and particularly in the striving after dramatic effect which they evince. And perhaps it was he who designed the ' chariot ' with the ' Temptation of the Hermit ', which harked back to the extremely popular subject of the ' Temptations of St Anthony ', and which, according to the Brotherhood's records, was a great success.

It is, clearly, not easy to describe the cultural circles in which Bosch moved; they were undoubtedly very familiar with the literature, both esoteric and popular, of alchemy and magic. A society which delighted in the *Ars Moriendi* – the most superstitious work imaginable, even though it has realistic passages and is inspired by a profound faith, absurdly disguised as a detailed technical treatise – was undoubtedly a complex and troubled one. In this society, alchemy was considered to be an acceptable and widespread means of spiritual fulfilment; a doctrine which answered a deeply felt need (discounting the rare, disparate, and distorted theories of a still embryonic experimental science). It became suspect only when it adopted the forms and actual methods of black magic, and was thus transformed into a vehicle for satanic ideas. This was the period when Innocent VIII issued the famous Bull *Summis desiderantes affectibus* (1484) to combat the growing spread of magical practices; the period, too, in which appeared, three years later, the terrible *Malleus maleficarum,* which was to have such significance in the Inquisition as a guide to trials for witchcraft. Even the most orthodox Catholic circles were pervaded by currents of thought, and moral attitudes, inconceivable at any other period. A number of famous preachers, such as Alain de la Roche, conveyed their ideas by means of apocalyptic but obscenely pornographic images; they hoped to add to their persuasive power by an appeal to the imagination of their listeners. In the same way, they made polemical use, though indirectly, of the alchemical view of the universe, which (in contrast to that of its opponents) saw the basic distinction between male and female constantly reflected, and interpreted marriage as the fundamental reintegration of reality. Church buildings had become the scene of meetings of all kinds; even courtesans were to be found there, in search of casual clients (see J. Huizinga, *The Waning of the Middle Ages*, Harmondsworth 1950), while processions and pilgrimages served – more often than is realized – to prepare the spirit for further sins while relieving it of earlier burdens of guilt. Moral instability and uncertainty is the heavy toll which generations living in times of transition are bound to pay.

And it is because of this very instability that the psychological enigma of Bosch remains unsolved. Whatever its ultimate solution may be, it provides a forceful reminder of the complexity of the human personality – the violence of men's fears, the corruption, the bestiality, which can only partially be hidden under the superficial respectability, the social rank and function, which screen them. Bosch's message – though it is embodied in art of the highest order – could also be that of an Adamite, according to the view of Wilhelm Fraenger (*Die Hochzeit zu Kana: Ein Dokument semitischer Gnosis bei Hieronymus Bosch,* Berlin 1950). On the other hand, the painter's fantastic caprices – though strictly controlled by an outstanding sense of form and composition – may well be the result of a dream-like abnormal experience, or of hallucinations produced by the use of some drug. R. L. Delevoy (*Bosch*, Geneva 1960, p. 76) points out that various cures which doctors carried out with a 'witches' oiñtment' (of which the formula was published in a sixteenth-century book, and which caused a sensation when it was discovered) produced in a number of subjects hallucinations extraordinarily similar to those of Bosch's weird world. This is not to decry either the value of his work or the creative power of his genius; but it does, none the less, allow the possibility that the artist may have made use of this and other similar means to stimulate his imagination, already animated by deep religious feeling.

Visionary experience, with its revelation of the negative, demoniacal aspects of the human personality, and of the constant presence of evil in even the most serene character, may enable us to approach the divine and sublime elements with greater concentration and awareness. And perhaps Bosch is the only artist who has succeeded in expressing both aspects equally forcefully. Yet the doubt remains. And very striking paradoxes also remain, whatever the truth may be – particularly as the notorious androgyny of the Adamites throws light on a number of obscure facets of his symbolism and his work. Bosch's artistic personality was undoubtedly a disturbed one, which oscillated, perhaps unconsciously, between opposite poles; it was, however, clearly imbued with its own mystical validity, which Bosch conveys in his painting through symbols and through a style which is exceptionally coherent and well-balanced. And – as José de Sigüença, the seventeenth-century commentator and apologist for Bosch, observed – he had the courage to paint man as he really is in the inner depths of his nature. The fact that this view of humanity, which allowed him to express obsessive fantasies, temptations, all the grotesque aspects of the human psyche, was dependent upon a system of values which accepted the reality of damnation, is today one of minor relevance. Everyone may form his own interpretation, according to his own particular tenets – provided that he has sufficient courage to look into himself and recognize – at least in part – his reflection in the magic mirror of a master's art.

Works

All the extant works by Bosch are entirely devoid not only of any date, but also of direct or indirect chronological references. Critics have had to rely on psychological elements and on content, as well as on stylistic evidence, and there is now almost universal agreement in recognizing the existence of four main periods. The first comprises the five-year period from 1475 to 1480, while the second centres on the turn of the century; the third (which was the most fruitful) was a very few years later (1504-5), and the last just preceded his death. This is an arbitrary division, for the sake of convenience, which certainly has a basis of truth but leaves a large margin for discussion (especially with the transitional phases); such uncertainty is inevitable, given the lack of dates and the loss of a great many paintings. Besides, Bosch has borne the burden of the interest which his fantasies and symbolism have aroused; genuinely constructive stylistic research, studying the images and meanings which animate the world of his paintings, has been subordinated to the pursuit of the ephemeral phantom of his personality, made yet more elusive by strained and often erroneous interpretation.

The group of early paintings unquestionably contains themes which recur later, in a far more complex form. As far as style is concerned, Bosch seems to be entirely original, ready-formed – though with a streak of archaism which is not, in fact, the expression of a provincial backwardness (such as one might justifiably expect to find in the prevailing cultural context of 's Hertogenbosch), but appears to be deliberate and intentional. One might perhaps come across echoes of the style of his grandfather, Jan van Acken, stylistic mannerisms derived from currents which really were provincial, and reminiscences – even striking ones – of the miniaturists who flourished at the beginning of the fifteenth century. But the archaism is, nevertheless, the result of a clear and definite stylistic attitude which distinguishes Bosch from the prevalent Flemish taste of his time. At first, he was interested in the *external* manifestations of man – in the darker aspects of his personality, or the spitefulness and stupidity which govern social intercourse. That is what chiefly concerned him, though already he was preparing esoteric iconographic and structural formulae, complex symbolic schemata which would later be developed at length.

In his concern to delineate sins and weaknesses, to pinpoint the wiles of malice (or of the Devil, who is not, as yet, clearly distinguishable in the vagueness and confusion), and in his attempt to clarify the uncertainties and contradictions of the human personality, Bosch drew his inspiration from real life, from the external world, from the society of his time. And moreover he introduced a new kind of landscape – spacious, open, serene; utterly different from the kind of composition usually adopted at the time. With the *Seven Deadly Sins* (painted around 1475), he began the long series of *genre* scenes in northern painting; though the design is clearly based on magic and symbolism (*pls. 1-8*). Indeed, the *tondi* in the corners, of the Four Last Things (Death, the Last Judgement, Hell, Paradise), mark a square within which the central circle – closely surrounding a ring emitting rays which encloses the figure of the resurrected Christ and which bears the inscription: CAVE, CAVE, DEUS VIDET (' Beware, beware, God sees ') – forms a perfect *mandala* (to use an Indian word which has now come into general use, meaning ' a circle ', and which actually implies

9

a highly complex mental picture of the world). Like the Indian *mandala*, Bosch's painting is designed to bring about, in successive stages, a full awareness of the spiritual truth embodied in the centre.

Here, the world (or rather society), confined within the boundaries of the journey we must all make and its inevitable end (either reward or punishment), seems to be pervaded with evil. Yet Christ, risen again, is always there – the pivot of the whole world, its supreme hope, and the symbolic embodiment of the Eye of God which sees and judges all.

It is not suprising that this painting is so widely admired, both for its imaginative impact and its stylistic clarity; nor is the analogy with the Buddhist *mandala* to be wondered at, since both have their roots in ancient magical tradition. Paradise, and the Apotheosis of Christ the King (a demon attempts to seize a woman and drag her away, contrasting with an angel's red cross), Hell with its pitchforks, its tortures, its monstrous devils and fantastic landscapes – these give a foretaste, however mild, of Bosch's later works.

The Conjuror (in Saint-Germain-en-Laye), silhouetted against a wall redolent of ruin and desolation, on which are thrown, in faint perspective, the shadows of the crowd and of the table – he, in contrast, glows in a fiery, demonic robe, the colour of bull's blood. Various examples of humanity are watching him – or rather are watching the spellbound, stooping old fool whose purse is being stolen by an *insouciant* companion; the old man is raising his eyes to the skies above a ridiculous pair of pince-nez, while a child laughs. The frog on the table, the owl half-hidden in the basket, the dog (or monkey) with the clown's hat, are the symbolic expressions of credulity, heresy, the vile and ridiculous aspect of demonic power, which is here still that of the mere magician, and is thus very far from the sinister complexities of the later works.

The Cure of Folly (*pls. 9-10*), with its wide evening landscape, is accompanied, or rather framed, by the inscription in fine Gothic lettering: MEESTER SNIJT DIE KEIE RAS, MIJNE NAME IS LUBBERT DAS, 'Master, take away the stone in haste; my name is *Lubbert Das*' (meaning a 'stupid idiot'). The stone (*keie*) is the 'stone of madness'. That the 'Master' is a quack, a charlatan, is shown by the funnel which he wears as a hat – a symbol of deceit which often recurs in Bosch's work. Armed with a large scalpel, and assisted by a monk who appears to have faith in him, he is watched closely by a woman, a nun, who balances a closed book precariously on her head. In the background, almost merging into the serene landscape, are a gallows and a wheel. The whole scene – which is basically a genre painting, apart from its situation – speaks of deceit, treachery, and human folly, but without overt allusions, except for the general atmosphere of strangeness which suffuses the indifference of nature.

This is the point where many interpretations – even the most highly esteemed – come to grief. Perhaps Bosch wants to tell us that it as a fool's game to attempt to get rid of that grain of madness which everyone has, and which gives life a certain zest; it is better to have something to believe in and keep the book of truth closed, rather than open it and read it – if it is in fact written.

The *Vagabond* (in the Boymans Museum, Rotterdam), though a more complex and profound work, showing far greater maturity and a very different kind of sensitivity, is nevertheless linked with this first group of works belonging to the artist's youth. For some critics this work, which is without any question one of the greatest paintings in the world, seems to be a late one and to belong to the last years of the master's life; while other critics, on the contrary, consign it to his full maturity – in fact, shortly after the first of the great triptychs, *The Hay-wain*. The mastery of the techniques of expression, the subtle gradations of tone, the balance of the composition, point to an advanced stage in Bosch's artistic development. But the relative rarity of symbols, the fact that the work is based on a sturdy realism, and that – whatever the true significance of the painting may be – it is fundamentally a genre scene: these facts relate the painting to the early works, either in direct continuity with them or as a not unaccountable return to earlier themes, if it is in fact a late work. The main figure – ragged, but not poor (as his bulging purse proves) –

is leaving a strange, tumbledown house. A weapon (a dagger) and an amulet (a hare's foot) serve to protect him. His face, which is prematurely old, with huge, animated eyes, expresses the dilemma of the man who hesitates between the pleasures of the world (of which he is now weary) and the way of the Lord. Whatever he represents – whether he is simply a 'vagabond' or the Prodigal Son, or an allegory of Free Will, he is certainly the symbol of anguished mankind, weighed down with the burden of heresy (the owl on the branch). Incidental details, sometimes emphatic (such as that of the man beneath the inn-sign), bring out the psychological implication of this breathless climb up the steep path; the pigs at their trough seem to confirm that this is indeed a parable of the Prodigal Son. But if this was, in fact, the chosen subject, it has been interpreted with such an obvious psychological bias and in such precise detail (though occasionally a little whimsical, as with the shoes) that it involves a kind of fantastic realism. It provides, as it were, a ruthless analysis of human uncertainty when faced with contrasting values that man's conscience can accept or reject only with the greatest difficulty. And here, too, man is the central figure.

In the triptych of the 'Hay-wain' (pls. 12-23), where a more complex symbolism begins to appear [and where on the back of the folding leaves (pl. 12) there is a prefiguration of the Rotterdam Vagabond – the Prodigal Son – which is the crucial image of the whole painting], the action involves humanity as a whole. On the left, the painting shows the Fall of the Rebel Angels, who are reduced to a swarm of vile insects, winged salamanders, devils with bats' wings, hurled down by the might of Christ 'Pantocrator' into the water of a lake, or on to the ground (pl. 13). A rock with a vaguely human profile represents the petra genetrix, the 'mother stone', inanimate embodiment of a latent vitality extending even to the mineral kingdom, and which thus – even if it does spout the Water of Life – is in the last resort a potential receptacle for evil. The Creation of Eve, the Temptation (pl. 16), and the final banishment of the human couple from the Garden of Eden, complete the left-hand panel (pl. 17). But the creation of Eve (which is performed by the Father, wrapped in a red cloak, with a kind of mitre on his head) is arranged according to a liturgical (or perhaps even magical) scheme, very different from the simple act of creation.

The central panel, from which the painting as a whole derives its title, alludes to the Flemish proverb in which hay figures as the symbol of wealth, of avidity, and of the passions which it arouses. 'All is but hay'; the wain, drawn by a group of grotesquely bestial monsters, lashed by a tree-man with dry, thorny branches, wreaks havoc among the crowd as it passes – fierce and futile struggles where everyone tries (usually in vain) to grab as much hay as possible. A crack in an absurd hillock, surmounted by a mushroom which repeats the motif of the egg, also disgorges more people, among them a number of Orientals, and behind the wain comes the majestic but tragic procession of the world's great ones, drawn in the wake of the Devil's chariot towards their damnation (*pl. 20*). In the foreground are genre scenes – the blind man with a boy as his guide, the charlatan with his science (*pl. 19*), and the fat friar to whom nuns are bringing armfuls of hay. On the wain two pairs of lovers appear between a kneeling angel and a devil who plays some infernal melody while he dances. These, like the other figures, have as their background the Tree of Life, and a wide, unreal, luminous landscape tinged with blue, over which hangs the golden cloud which signifies the glory of Christ. The vase (symbol of female sexuality) and the owl (symbol of heresy), suspended on either side of the tree, complete the composition.

On the right-hand panel, silhouetted against livid, inextinguishable flames, jut the ruined, smoking, fantastic buildings of a Hell which rests on a bridge spanning a monstrous sewer. The naked bodies of the sinners stand out against the black and bluish shapes of the devils bound to torments that give them satisfaction, engaged in senseless activity, using crazy scaffolding intended perhaps for some incredible torture (*pls. 21-3*). The path of evil, from its triumphant birth to its perverse, wished-for punishment, is here shown in its entirety – just as Bosch's world of fantasy is now entirely complete.

Themes such as that of ecclesiastics ruined by sin (seduced by the Devil's wiles) are not in themselves in the least heretical; and perhaps they have not, either, any strictly satirical implications – even when they take the form of a caricature. Rather, they are reflections of a commonplace in literature – both mystical (as with Ruysbroeck) and humanistic. But from the time of this first great painting (actually the weakest stylistically of those which have come down to us), Bosch's world is fully formed, even though many of the themes which he later cultivated to the point of obsession are still absent. What is certain – as is proved by, among other things, the fish with legs, or the tree-man driving the hay-wain – is that Bosch's world-view diverges from traditional lines. It assumes the appearance of an ' anti-world ', which is out of joint, and in which – like some startling reflection of the gradual conquest of the objective, real world which the civilization of his time was accomplishing – the works of man's hand seem to take on a life of their own and turn against him. Architectural perspectives are distorted by crumbling buildings on every side, while normally lifeless objects are imbued with life, or mingled with the most monstrous forms of animal life. Evil is everywhere, since human activity, seduced by the Devil's wiles, carries and infuses it everywhere.

The *Ship of Fools* (*pl. 11*) is of a different type; it dates, probably, from a little later than 1494, the year in which appeared the literary work of the same title by Sebastian Brant. This painting shows, beneath a banner with the new moon – a reference to the antithesis between Catholicism and Islam – the theme of the mad monk and friar enjoying the pleasures of this world (the lute has a clear erotic significance, and so have the cherries on the plate); the motif of the ' Tree of Cockaigne ' also occurs here – for the ship's mast is a real tree, with branches and leaves. The owl and the oar – which is in fact a ladle – together with those symbols of madness, the bowl and the long, curved stick with a skull on the end, complete the symbolism of this painting, which is as intricate as a miniature, and which, with its concern for effects of light and shade, presages the horrific faces in the *Ascent to Calvary* in Ghent.

And the theme of the ship ought perhaps to be seen in relation to Erasmus's *In Praise of Folly* (1501).

The obsession with evil, the pressure of the magical influences which develop and control it, appears even more clearly in the *Marriage at Cana* (*pl. 34*). For Fraenger, this painting, packed with symbolism, is openly heretical. But if we see it in the context of Bosch's whole *oeuvre,* while it may well allude to the rites and influence of the believers in Free Will (Fraenger considers that it was the Grand Master of the sect who persuaded Bosch to paint it), this may be only in order to point out how evil forces penetrate, of their own accord, even the most sacred moments – even when Christ is performing the miracle. Christ himself, against a background of a golden panel decorated in Islamic style, is blessing the pyx, which is open since the cover is on the table, and which a strange figure, with reddish head of hair and clothed in robes which resemble magic vestments, is presenting to the bride and groom. In the background a magician, holding a wand and standing in front of a cabinet which is also a magic altar, is beginning to perform a magic rite, and the food is coming to life, is transformed into poisonous monsters. Thus the whole scene (apart from Christ and the pensive old man on his left) is suffused with magic, while death stares in from the garden. Bosch's style is now free of any awkwardness; this most unconventional of paintings, rich in arcane allusions, shows an unusual familiarity with magic ritual – and, more important, emphasizes the isolation of Christ, who dominates the group yet remains outside it. Perhaps Bosch's message here is merely that of an ironic extension, even to the Redeemer himself, of the idea of ' one crying in the wilderness ', with no overt blasphemous intentions. He seems to want to minimize the persuasive force of a truth which is constantly stifled by the forces of evil.

The *Marriage at Cana* is among the best and most complex of Bosch's works, but his artistic powers reach their peak with the magnificent *Adoration of the Magi* in the Prado (*pls 24-33*), in which the theme of evil lying in wait recurs again. This painting is a complex, highly wrought figurative poem, dominated by the landscape; on the horizon are detailed, fantastic buildings, somehow unreal, shot through with biblical and classical references. Bosch confers on them a sense of life hidden within inanimate walls, which themselves suggest astonished faces. Melchior is on his knees, Balthasar is standing (*pl. 25*); as king of Godolia and Sheba, he wears on his short cloak, worked in relief, the scene of the Visit of the Queen of Sheba to Solomon, which prefigures the Epiphany. His crown (under which the toads of heresy are squatting), laid at the Virgin's feet, is decorated with statues representing the Sacrifice of Abraham, a prefiguration of the Crucifixion (*pl. 29*). Behind stands Caspar (*pl. 24*), the Moorish king of Tarsis, who is offering myrrh in a round casket (*pl. 28*).[1] The scene in the foreground – the Virgin with the Child, the Three Magi, two donors accompanied by St Peter and St Agnes – forms a liturgical group, anticipating the Mass. The Virgin is the altar, and the Child the consecrated Host; Melchior is the celebrant, and the other Magi his acolytes. The widespread knowledge of the work by Hildesheim on the Magi, and the existence of a special rite, the Rouen ' office of the three kings ', *Officium regum trium secundum usum Rothomagensem,* give scope for an interpretation of this kind. The presence of various symbols is less easily explicable: that of licentiousness on Melchior's crown (*pl. 29*); the hawk pecking at a cherry (another symbol of sensuality – see *pl. 28*) on the round casket containing myrrh (on which is engraved the scene of the Gift of the Three Mighty Men to David – another prefiguration of the Epiphany); the metal berry attached by a twisted cord to the globe itself. Such symbols seem to allude to the journey of the Magi from the human world to that of redemption (see also Lotte Brand-Philip, in *The Art Bulletin,* 1953, pp. 267-93), since here too everything is pervaded by evil. There are the three armies of the Magi; the one at the ford next to the bridge seems to be composed of Mongols, to judge by their costumes, and may be a covert allusion to the punitive attack by the Mongols (the people of Prester John) on a Europe submerged in sin, which corresponds to both Western and Oriental traditions about the evangelical Magi. There are, too, the juggler moving away; the somersaulting acrobat carved on the doorway of the ruined building where St Joseph is drying linen cloths (*pl. 32*); the white statue of Hermes Trismegistus; the staff tipped with a crescent moon, which an idiot (*pl. 33*) is balancing on his head; the wild boar; the man attacked by a wolf; the women fleeing from another wolf; the broken staff which indicates the disruption of magical protection. All these are signs referring to the magical-demonic world which suffuses the landscape. Even in the hut lurk ambiguous creatures. A strange figure, half naked despite his red cloak, with a mitre and a golden chain binding his right arm, with his leg held in a trap, may be a representation of the Hebrew Messiah; he is certainly, however, a clear allusion to Antichrist (*pl. 31*). Various figures, including Negroid Mongolians, move around behind him, while on the roof of the shepherds' hut the wicked shepherds spy upon the scene, hoping to reap some profit from it by their trickery (one clutches his bagpipes, another wears a dagger fixed in his leather cap, while the third, clambering up a tree, has a trap fastened to his waist).

Apart from *The Garden of Earthly Delights* (*pls. 60-79*), which is perhaps Bosch's masterpiece, and which reveals new and different symbolic aspects, a number of sources of inspiration can be singled out – to be distinguished by the choice of subject – in the remaining works. In the life of Christ, what interests Bosch (with the exception of the Brussels *Crucifixion*) is the mob's incomprehension, its cruelty, its inner rage. The crowd is made up of a varying number of figures, whose grotesque faces would be like caricatures, if they were not composed of hatred and derision. And – even more than violence – what strikes Bosch is man's idiotic, blind, brutish inability to acknowledge truth and justice. Here we are presented with the absurd drama of deicide seen from humanity's point of view – and also with the splendour of the divine sacrifice which redeems humanity and offers it salvation.

The second thread of inspiration concerns the cycle of the *Temptations of St Anthony,* in which merge a number of diverse strands, but which allows Bosch once more to emphasize the power of the forces of evil, and the isolation of holiness. Thus in a single strain, the *St Jerome* at Ghent, the *St John the Baptist in the Wilderness* in Madrid, as well as the *St John the Evangelist on Patmos* in Berlin (Dahlem), all converge.

Bosch did not trace the cycle of the *Temptations of St Anthony* solely (as did some of the artists who preceded and followed him) because it could give the artist freedom to represent what subject he chose (even scabrous themes that would otherwise be forbidden or subject to suspicion). For Bosch there were no forbidden ways, no boundaries, since he succeeded in portraying even the magic reversal of the Creed in the *Marriage at Cana*. But, apart from Bosch's predilection for the fantastic and the monstrous, apart from his ability to lay bare certain aspects of the human heart, he is probing, even in the *Temptations,* into the burden of evil, the negative power which mingles with the very flux of life, and which seems to be inseparable from it — unless with infinite effort the individual succeeds in merging his personality with the divine essence.

And here we rejoin the third thread of inspiration. For it is not only Hell and the Last Judgment that fascinate Bosch, but also — and perhaps even more — Paradise. The panel in the Palazzo Ducale in Venice, showing the *Ascent to the Empyrean,* if taken on its own, gives the impression of reliving a personal experience undergone by (or at least understood by) the artist (*pl. 39*).

The clear and slender bodies of the blessed, supported by many-coloured angels possessed of an inner radiance (which is obtained by a special preparatory technique) climb, against a background of shadows and grey clouds, towards a vast tunnel of 'solidified' light (as in paranormal experiences), ringed with rib vaulting. It is thus both a hollow cylinder seen in perspective (reminiscent of the Hermetic Mercury), and also a geometric composition which alludes to the position of the successive Heavens relative to the earth. The souls which are there have lost every trace of corporeal weight; they have become light, slender beings, bathed in the light of the divine essence, without face or form, such as one imagines beyond the passage which will bear one through all superficial appearances, all relative phenomena, to an eternal Absolute, motionless, inexpressible. Many aspects of Bosch's work have a parallel in the mystical experience of people in every era and every country. The confrontation with the Divine Light, the abandonment of self in the vortex of light which first clarifies and then transfigures, at sunrise and sunset, the being who is involved – these are experiences which belong to every age and every faith. But Bosch's art succeeds in communicating them – so far as is humanly possible – to the infinite ranks of those who will never, during their mortal existence, experience mystical ecstasy at first hand. [2] No work of art, of East or West, has been able to convey the inexpressible with such clarity, simplicity and power.

These, then, are the chief paths that Bosch's genius followed. And so far as the first of these (the theme of the Passion of Christ) is concerned, this may have a theatrical origin, which can be observed in (among other things) the emphasis on perspective in his compositions, as in a stage set; and the exaggerated facial characterization of the figures, such as those in the *Ecce Homo* at Frankfurt (*pl. 44*). But the faces of the chief figures also express an increasing modification and intensification of the feelings which the painter embodies – often in a violent way – throughout his work; from first to last his paintings seem dominated by a deep, sincere disgust with humanity, unable to rise above its own passions.

From the four figures in the *Christ Mocked* (*The Crowning with Thorns*) in London (*pl. 41*), who are callously crushing innocence with the power of their armed strength – mocking at it with an esoteric demoniacal knowledge (the old man on the left has a crescent moon on the cloak which covers his head), or battering at it with rough force (like the grotesque bourgeois on the right); from this painting right up to the darkness of the *Ascent to Calvary*, peopled with monstrous, sneering faces, with creatures who represent the whole of humanity (from the Negro to Mongolian), Bosch's development follows a course which is, according to R. L. Delevoy, unique in the history of art. In any case, it is exceptional, inasmuch as it reflects an alteration in the artist's attitude to life – a growing pessimism, an ever more desperate view of the world. The *Ascent to Calvary* in Ghent (*pls. 46-7*), with the sorrowing Christ, Veronica, and the firm-featured Simon of Cyrene merging into the shadowy background – above all the Good Thief, who is being subjected to the fanatical, moralizing reproaches of a hideous friar – this is in effect a devastating indictment of a society which not only is ignorant of goodness and generosity but does not hesitate to cloak injustice and fraud in the garments of the sacred. In Christ's inner sorrow, and in the Good Thief's terror, is there some reflection of a personal ordeal (completely unknown biographically)? If we were not aware of Bosch's amazing imaginative resources, we might well think so, for it seems impossible that the anguish of a man subject to an unjust charge could be conveyed in a clearer or more telling way.

Here, however, we must confine ourselves simply to noting that Bosch is self-absorbed – that up to the end of his life he sought the themes of his art in his own psyche; we may perhaps find confirmation of this development towards an ever-deeper withdrawal into himself, in another of the themes which inspired him – that of the *Temptations of St Anthony*. For the last of the paintings which survive, which must date from 1515 (*pls. 48-9*), shows the saint crouching in a shelter made from a hollow tree-trunk, indifferent to – and, as it were, detached from – the onslaught of the demons. It is as if his eyes were fixed on some vision which distracted him from the imminent attack, and which nullified the external reality around him. Yet Bosch's imagination has lost nothing of its power or inventiveness. The tower which has come to life, with monkeys' paws and human arms, covered with a funnel which hides its unspeakable entrails, is in fact one of the most perfect examples of the fusion of the inanimate with the animate. And the face of the clawed creature floating on the surface of the muddy water (*pl. 49*), which the saint does not notice, is closely linked, in intensity of expression if not in actual style, to the *Ascent* in Ghent (*pls. 46-7*). Bosch sets out to express the distorting influence of hatred and mockery. However, in the evolutionary sequence of Bosch's *Temptations of St Anthony*, we come across works which spring from an imaginative impulse that is far more vital and, as it were, far less introspective, than the one we have just been considering. The *Temptation* in Lisbon (*p. 23*) is the finest example of this; it is a doctrinal statement which – though obscure to us – was clearly intended to be wholly explicit. It is possible that the *Temptations of St Anthony,* which flourished, as a literary form, in an Oriental context (that of Coptic Christianity), contain, as Jurgis Baltruishaitis considers they do, Buddhist allusions. The attack by Mara, the god of life and love, on the future Buddha, as he meditates below the Tree of Illumination, on the night before the conquest of Truth resembles the *Temptation of St Anthony* in many ways. And life's deceptions – the ebb and flow of desires and feelings – when judged as works of the Devil (that is, snares for wisdom and holiness) are expressed in similar forms in Buddhist and Christian tradition.

The *Temptation* in Lisbon deliberately introduces a new element into the theme of the *Temptation of St Anthony,* with a wealth of symbolic and doctrinal implications. The whole composition, in fact, hinges upon an oblique, rather short axis, which runs from the Crucifix in the dark chapel to the ruined building (beside the actual presence of Christ, who is in the act of blessing). Passing across the saint's countenance (he is looking at the observer), it comes to an end in the magic sign spread out on the ground in front of a magician in a red cloak. This is a transposition, a modernization (relative to Bosch's time) of the theme of temptation, seen as the conflict between the ability to turn to one's own advantage the occult forces of the universe, and the Christian reliance on the reality of faith.

Bosch's paintings are a denunciation of magic by a man who believes deeply in its existence and its power, who sees the world of magic as a deceptive but seductive truth. This is shown by the images which adorn the ruined tower-pillar of the tottering building; among other things, they range from obvious, unreal symbolic and moralizing images, to the unexpectedly realistic appearance of a sheet of water which reveals genuine perspectives within the wall itself.

The purely moralistic content of Bosch's work – if ever there was one – appears to undergo a modification at this point on his career; for from now on he turns his back on the unnatural and confines his attacks to a sin which is not incompatible with a perfectly creditable impulse. Perhaps we are looking for excessively clearcut interpretations of works which are highly complex and strange; or it may be that the extreme monotony of our own epoch compels us to search even in the smallest details (often vainly) for meaning and allusions which Bosch might have contrived. However this may be, the theme of temptation — even when not expressed with such a wealth of obscure details — is undeniably one that recurs constantly in his work. We come across it again in the *St John the Baptist* in the Museo Lázaro-Galdiano, Madrid (*pl. 56*), where the plant growing next to the saint, with its huge pod split open and pecked at by a bird, looks like a kind of vegetable serpent, a misshapen monster with weird tentacles. It is, without any doubt, an assertion of the power of evil inherent in life and in nature. Similarly, the theme of the opposition between evil and holiness recurs in the *St. Jerome in Penitence,* the central panel of the *Altarpiece of the Hermits* in Venice (*pl. 55*), which has a wealth of astrological and other symbols, such as the falling statue or the tame unicorn, which occur nowhere else in Bosch's work. The same central theme recurs in the *St Jerome at Prayer,* in Ghent (*pls. 52-3*). Even the apparently serene painting of *St John the Evangelist on Patmos,* quite apart from its reference to the writing of the Apocalypse, is haunted by a demon with a sad, pale face, grotesquely embodied in the apparently fragile form of a fat, absurd insect.

But the most complex, fully realized, and — from our point of view — mysterious painting of all, is certainly still the triptych of the *Garden of Earthly Delights* (*pls. 60-79*). Even more than the terrifying *Last Judgment* at Vienna (*pls. 35-37*), this painting seems to focus all the enigmas of Bosch's mind; to decipher these, and accurately interpret their ambiguous aspects, would be to put to flight all the shadows oppressing the personality of this extraordinary creator of monsters and fantasies, to throw light on some of the paradoxes of his character, and above all to learn the fears, and possibly the guilt, which form an integral part of it. For, although the general significance of the painting is almost certainly that which is traditionally ascribed to it, it is still doubtful to what extent the condemnation of sensuality is a sincere and genuinely felt one. What actual experiences lie behind it? Is there not a particular satisfaction inherent in the treatment of these ethereal nudes — fleshy yet almost weightless, fantastic yet realistic? In any case, the accumulation of esoteric symbols is both obscure and (in some respects) apparently paradoxical.

The Temptation of St Anthony, Lisbon (*see note on p. 39*)

The closed shutters of the triptych represent a particular moment in the creation of the world (*pl. 60*), which is seen as a sphere the upper half of which is crystalline, allowing us a glimpse of the formation of the world and of plant life; an apocalyptic light – livid, stormy, – filters through a mass of clouds bunched high in the sky. The vegetable forms – rather hard to distinguish – which seem to grow out of the earth like grotesque solidifications, already sometimes have shapes which are unnatural, literally 'monstrous'. They confirm that the forces of evil are inherent in creation itself, in an indissoluble and inseparable conjunction of opposites; and they also indicate that nature contains more mysteries than are dreamed of by human reason. Like a real obsession, the form of the crystal sphere recurs several times, though with different meanings, within this painting, in which we pass from the *Creation of Eve* in the Garden of Eden, which is surmounted by the Fountain of Youth, (formed of pink coral and composed of shapes which are evidence of the fluidity of the frontier between the animal and the vegetable worlds, between the animate and the inanimate: *pl. 61*) – to the so-called 'musical inferno' (*pls. 76-9*).

The central panel, the largest, is an ambiguous composition which may perhaps express the pleasures of a life free of restraint, or the infinite succession of temptations, and which yet succeeds in conveying in the most decorative and deeply poetic form the innermost springs of human nature – its insatiable longings, its anxieties, and its ridiculous illusions.

The entire left-hand panel, showing the *Creation of Eve*, pivots on the spherical base of the *Fountain of Youth,* which is placed precisely at the centre of the actual panel. Because of its shape, and because of the hole in its centre (where an owl is nesting), the sphere assumes the horrible fixity of an eye which registers the presence of evil (*pl. 65*). In the foreground, Christ presents Eve to Adam, who is just waking up; but the tree behind them – the Tree of the Knowledge of Good and Evil – assumes a strange tuberous shape, probably a reference to the evil powers contained in the vegetable kingdom (*pl. 64*). The rocks above, pierced and twisted, give shelter to wheeling flocks of rooks. The landscape is inhabited by animals of every kind, imaginary and grotesque or genuine, deriving from medieval bestiaries (as with the monstrous giraffe) or from the observation of reality (as with the cat holding a mouse in his mouth, below the fateful tree – an allusion to human weakness). These creatures inspire a sense of some subtly malevolent unreality and ambiguity. The Garden of Eden is already touched with evil, destined for corruption.

The central panel (*pl. 63*), divided into three contiguous sections – one above the other, as in medieval tapestries – is peopled exclusively with animals, either real or imaginary (nearly always symbolic) and with naked human beings. A single figure is shown clothed – half-hidden, at the bottom, by a group of naked women and by a large glass tube which seems to emerge from a cleft in the earth. On the identity of this figure depends, in all probability, the exact meaning of the painting as a whole (*pl. 72*). It has been suggested that he is the Grand Master of the Adamites; the man who may have commissioned, and even (as Fraenger postulates) supervised, Bosch's work, suggesting to him both the content and the symbolism of the actual paintings. But, although it is undeniable that the *Garden of Earthly Delights* is a thing apart, in many respects, in Bosch's *oeuvre,* it is also inconceivable that Bosch should have wished – or been able – to conform to any other person's ideas. Whoever the clothed man may be who is instructing the woman with sealed lips (the very essence *in vitro* of every form of femininity), the painting as a whole is undoubtedly the fruit of Bosch's own imagination. The proportions are symbolic: certain birds are shown as huge in size, compared with humans, and this is clearly linked to certain obsessive, or at least, dominant themes. The owls have a sinister significance, and embody precise allusions to either heresy or magical-alchemical forces. The real woodpecker, the mallard, the kingfishers, and of course the peacock, also have magical meanings; these vary according to the currents of esoteric thought but are usually allied to folk tales, proverbs, or alchemical speculations (*pl. 75*). Similarly, the fruit which people are eating has a symbolic significance – always connected with the pleasures of the flesh, and in particular with lust. The presence of Negro men and women, of tubes (*pl. 73*), and of glass phials, is an allusion both to erotic pleasure and to alchemy – for ' the eye of the heart can see gold (the symbol of God) in lead, and crystal within the mountain! ' – and, in general, to the universality of magic and alchemy. [3]

It has been suggested that this triptych is designed to serve as an aid to meditation, and that the recurrent motif of the sphere is intended to aid concentration and help to induce an autohypnotic trance state. But I think that it is intended to aid meditation purely through rational reflection on its difficult symbolism. Thus, in the upper section, the sphere in the centre of the lake (*pl. 61*), the source of the four rivers of earth (or of Paradise?), is a magic nucleus having, probably, important allusions to the moon; it is characterized by the presence of figures of acrobats; they were considered, at that time, to be endowed with magic and demonic powers, since they were able (at least apparently) to break the bounds and laws of nature (*pls. 66-7*). The couple standing on their hands give the hollow, cracked sphere, in the middle of the upper lake, a negative meaning, underlined by the new moon and the complicated glass structure which surmounts it. This is, clearly, a false Fountain of Life and Truth.

Some of those who are revelling in it, and drinking it, are attempting to enter and crowd together in the shell of a broken egg (the symbol of spiritual and doctrinal isolation, such as the alchemists knew); [4] the *vae solis* of the Bible sounds for each one of them. Others, blinded by passion and the lure of the senses (represented by the huge berry which another group holds in the air), estrange themselves from any way of life not ruled by pleasure.

Below is the round pool of the Spring of Youth (and which, with its slender elongated bathers, recalls medieval bathing scenes). Here a Negress carrying a peacock on her head and holding a cherry, combines the symbols of vanity and of licentiousness. The fair-haired girls on whom ravens – symbols of heretical doctrine and dialectic – are perching, complete the catalogue of female vice. All around circles the most fantastic and heterogeneous cavalcade of naked figures imaginable (*pl. 75*), mounted on griffons, unicorns (possibly evil, since the horn is branched), camels, wild boars, bears, blue panthers, deer, horses, donkeys, and goats (drawn from bestiaries and from the earliest accounts of the Far East); their significance may be linked to the complex symbolism of Ruysbroeck. Some of the riders are calm and dignified; others pair off with gestures and attitudes which clearly allude (however delicately) to physical union, or are engaged in acrobatic exercises which have obscene connotations.

The porcupine and the owl are the emblems of this procession, in which there twice recurs the motif of the fish (also as a spear, alluding to defloration); we come across it again in the extreme foreground of the central panel, as a dead trophy, the memorial to past pleasures. Almost at the geometric centre of the panel — actually at the crossing point of the diagonals of the whole triptych when open — the alchemical egg on the head of one of the riders marks the focal point of the whole composition. Whether it signifies the indefinite, the embryonic — the asexual seed from which springs a universe to which the key is seen as sexual (since even plants and stones are envisaged as male and female) — or whether it signifies as an alchemical crucible, the fact remains that the egg is a frankly heretical symbol so far as Catholicism is concerned. The more so as the symbolic meanings listed here are interconnected, and are basically variations on the same theme.

In the foreground — apart from the birds, the berries, the pods — groups of naked creatures perform unnatural actions in which the theme of carnal union, of frenzied sexuality, of perverted or illicit *eros,* is constantly present, from the wood which proffers fruit to the couples (but from the shadows emerges another man, who appears to be clothed), to the trio enclosed in the glass bell of an artificial flower (*pl. 68*); from the two dancers partly covered by an egg-shaped *corolla* surmounted by an owl, who recall Indian figures of dancing, many-armed deities (and even more the fabulous twins of medieval tradition and of books illustrating biological prodigies)[5] to the man head-downwards in the pool; another naked figure embraces an owl; a couple sit in a glass sphere which blossoms from a hollow, inhabited fruit into which the black rat, symbol of falsehood and pestilence, is summoned by a pallid man.

The group comprising the couple bound to an oyster shell which is closing upon them, and which a third person carries on his back (*pl. 71*); the groups who live inside fruits, or feed on berries – these complete this erotic fantasy, which to all appearances spells out every possible form (even pathological) of the human *eros,* all the states of mental disturbance caused by sexual excitement with or without the additional stimulus of drugs. The man whose head is changed into a berry (a symbol of the absolute dominance of the senses and fertility); the man who tempts a raven perching on his foot by offering him a cherry – these are overt allusions to the mental and physiological symptoms of unbridled sensuality. And on this theme Bosch's imaginative powers are indeed amazing. But the key to all the symbolism is held by the being – probably a demon, and at any rate endowed with magical knowledge – who emerges from a hole in the ground and who instructs the pale Eve with sealed mouth; for in the alchemical theory of sex (the glass tube dotted with round solar protuberances, *pl. 73*, is a clear reference to this) her powers are used to the detriment of humanity, becoming a destructive and negative force – if not actually a demoniacal one – as well as a source of life.

As we see, the alchemical egg is the centre of the composition, and its shifting and enigmatic symbolism is essential to the composition as a whole. Indeed, it occurs on all three of the panels, though with different functions and qualities, and in the third it predominates. The huge central figure (*pl. 77*) with a pale human face and a body like a broken, empty eggshell (enclosing a demon tavern) with arms like pigs' legs, transformed at the foot into hollow, dry treetrunks whose branches puncture its shell and thus wound its own spirit – this creature might be interpreted as a free rendering of the spherical androgyne envisaged by Plato. Though the image seems so unrealistic, it might have been produced by an unconscious combination of two mythical archetypes – the mundane egg and the primordial giant, but seen in the guise of an incubus and with symbolic allusions to sexual perversion. Thus the mill wheel which weighs down the head, symbolizing obsession, is surmounted by red bagpipes – a phallic symbol *par excellence*; the sexual reference is to sodomy, as is shown by the creature with an arrow stuck in the base of his spine, clambering up the ladder to reach the broken egg.

The theme of the hermaphrodite recurs, too, in the 'harp-lute'; a sinner is crucified to the strings of this imaginary instrument, which unites the tones and vibrations of male and female (*pl. 78*). The so-called 'musical inferno' (with the blue-shaded demon with a bird's head who swallows the damned, evacuating them from his own foul entrails, after extracting and releasing heretical ideas – the ravens) serves to express Hell with great force without scenes of torture. A rider who has fallen with his banner, the victim of monsters (the futility of courage?), a twisted corpse hanging in the eye of a huge key (the futility of culture?), while a raven (heresy) flies off into the distance – the rest of the painting embodies a grotesque obsession involving the whole of humanity (since the vast throng includes both Moors and Orientals).

Above, in the apocalyptic light of flames – which at times assume the dazzling brightness of a flare in a dark road-way – a city is being consumed (*pl. 76*). Armies are deserting it, crowds of men making their way towards it. Two huge human ears, joined by a bolt from a giant crossbow, hold the notched blade of a knife, and creep forward, devouring part of doomed mankind (*pl. 77*). The symbol is clearly phallic in form, but it is also an unanswerable indictment of those who, deceived by their senses, are deaf to the Word of God – the friar, trying to bring about the salvation of one of the men, confirms this interpretation. At the bottom, on the right, a naked man is receiving the embrace of a sow wearing a nun's cowl; on his knees lies a document (probably some heretical writing), while another figure – clothed in the roseate garb of heresy – carries two sealed envelopes. In front of them a monster formed from a helmet, with a severed foot hanging from the spiky crest – the same symbol which recurs in the demonic emblem in the Lisbon *Temptation* – advances, undeterred by the arrow which pierces its haunch. The allusion here is clearly to the demoniacal forces, in varying forms, which attack both the intellect and the senses of their victim.

A fuller analysis would require far more space, since no detail, however small, is ever haphazard; everything is more carefully wrought than in the most elaborate of miniatures. But is is possible to draw from the painting a significance which is both precise and penetrating. For essentially the triptych expresses the three most important moments in the alchemical process. The *Creation of Eve* is in effect the equivalent of the *Wedding*; the central panel represents the *Triumph of Love*; the 'Musical inferno' is *Death*. [6] These three phases correspond to the processes of ' combustion ', ' neutralization ', and ' incineration '; except that here the reference is to the human soul, sent towards love by God, but soiling and perverting love by giving it a hedonistic interpretation which bears within itself its own punishment.

Bosch presents an indictment of the decay of symbolism. He shows how the symbol of the primordial hermaphrodite, the undifferentiated life-force in which all conflicts are resolved, degenerates in the minds of the heretics of his age into a disgusting and incongruous sexual emblem. *Eros* declines to the level of a mere means to pleasure, and this decadence involves the extinction of the divine spark that exists in every man. The complex symbolism of the triptych – which is emphasized by the prevailing colour-scheme (pink and red are the colours of love, and blue is the colour of deception and of demons) – thus refers to the journey of the human spirit, wandering in a world where the pressure of the forces of evil is unremitting and omnipresent. Perhaps, in the right-hand panel, Bosch complements his central theme by a despairing vision of mankind as threatened with damnation both for the illusions of his senses and for the errors of his thought; this is Combe's hypothesis (in his *Jérôme Bosch,* 2nd ed., 1957, p. 34). But it is more than likely that, in the third panel of the *Garden of*

Delights, his intention was to express, not punishment in an after-life, but the anguish of the human being spent with pleasure and irredeemably severed from its original innocence.

The sense of sin weighs upon the whole triptych, although the artist delights in creating grotesque forms based on the seeds of beauty inherent in these same forms. *Mira quidem deformis formositas ac formosa deformitas* ('also admirable are ugly beauty and beautiful ugliness'), as Dionysius Certosinus said in the second half of the fifteenth century (*De venustate mundi et pulchritudine Dei, art. 9:* 'Quomodo ratio pulchri conveniat malis paenae et monstris'). His intention was to trace the slow decline of the spirit impelled by false doctrines – dazzled by an appearance of splendour – to interpret false (though spiritually exalted) ideological tenets by reducing them to their crudest sexual terms.

The battle against heresy became, for Bosch, an integral part of his nature. In this struggle, an important role was played by his knowledge both of alchemical theory and of the doctrines of hedonistic sects such as that of the Adamites. Witchcraft was, for him, a particularly important aspect of anti-religious thought: this is shown by the huge witch's head which merges with the hut rising out of the water in the second *Temptation of St Anthony* in the Prado (*pls. 50-1*). This painting is considered by some not to be authentic, but it is in fact certainly by Bosch (though not among his best works), at least so far as the saint's face and the hut with a human face are concerned. The landscape – very different from those which predominate in the later works – seems to be a return to the artist's earlier manner, in some aspects superseded after the Lisbon *Temptation*. For the rest, confirmation that the meaning of the so-called 'musical inferno' of the triptych of the *Delights* is as I have suggested, is provided by the different symbolic structure of the *Last Judgment* in Vienna (*pls. 35-37*). Here, both in the central panel (surmounted by the pallid radiance surrounding Christ Pantocrator and by the angels of the Judgment) and in the right-hand panel, the devils and torments are shown in a more grotesque and violent form – a water torture by the bridge; a great knife used to punish the lustful; other damned souls pierced with arrows. But basically this is a vision of the outside of things, the antechamber to Hell (*pl. 40*). True punishment lies beyond a door adorned with an endless string of toads, and watched by a devil whose grotesque face recalls – multiplied a hundredfold – the bestial and ferocious malevolence of Tibetan deities. Apart from the arrow at the end of his tail, this figure, armed with a grappling hook, his fiery entrails glimpsed through the grille of his stomach, recalls the incubi that the painters of Tibet conjure up from the unconscious with the aid of the contemplative methods of yoga. Probably this picture stems from hallucinations caused by drugs, for the similarity with contemporary Tibetan paintings is too marked to be merely accidental, though it cannot be in any way substantiated as an iconographic link. For this reason – while acknowledging that the left-hand part of the painting is very feeble – I feel justified in differing from Delevoy and other scholars who maintain that this is a copy of a lost original, carried out by a pupil, especially since either the copy is a perfectly faithful one (in which case certain divergences in the palette would still need explanation), or it is an arbitrary restoration. In the latter case, the symbolism (which introduces figures of insects, Dantesque symbols such as the snake-pit, and images of exceptional force such as the crippled demon with a basket) is too lively and varied to be attributable to a pupil such as the notoriously untalented Huys.

Let us assume, then, that the triptych is probably authentic, and that in it the earth's surface becomes an antechamber to the infernal punishments revealed by craters, flames, and flashes erupting on the surface. Thus it is not the fortunes of the human spirit, in life, that Bosch is here portraying, but the destiny of mankind as a whole, to the very end of time. This is shown in great – and ironic – clarity by the small numbers of the Blessed who accompany the figure of Christ. Though commonplace stylistically, the Vienna triptych is nevertheless of considerable significance iconographically, and for the light it throws on the meaning of Bosch's work as a whole.

It may be that the key to the mystery of Bosch's painting lies in his familiarity with, and experience of, anti-religious dogmas and theories, which nevertheless failed to destroy his faith. The pessimistic view of a world exposed, without possibility of escape, to the action of malevolent forces, impelled Bosch to represent, in preference to *post mortem* tortures, the triumphant forces of evil taking possession of this world, and the degeneration of the spirit and the intellect under their influence. Perhaps his sharpest insight is that man is horribly disfigured in life if he attempts to reach unattainable happiness by evil means. But perception of this kind could be acquired only by someone who had a profound familiarity with the magical doctrines of his day, and direct experience of them.

Bosch and the Critics

Bosch enjoyed considerable artistic success in his own life-time, as is shown by the appreciations noted in the records of the Brotherhood, and also by the fact that among his patrons was Philip the Handsome – who apparently ordered him to be paid 36 livres, in 1504, for a large *Last Judgment* (possibly that now in Munich); cf. *Registres de la Chambre des comptes de Lille,* 1504, Archives du Département du Nord, Reg. F. 190. On his death in 1516, two paintings (one showing the *Temptation of St Anthony*) appear in an inventory of the belongings of Margaret of Austria, Regent of the Netherlands. But the peak of popularity coincided (as J. Combe shows) with the peak of Spanish mysticism, and his reputation was particularly high in Spain. Several paintings were collected by Philip II and moved to the Escorial. Some of them came from the collection of Felipe de Guervara who, in his *Comentarios de la pintura* (c. 1560), published by A. Ponz in Madrid, deals fairly fully with Bosch, whom he greatly admires. Bosch had already been mentioned by Vasari (cf. G. Vasari, *Le vite dei più eccelenti pittori, scultori ed architettori,* Florence 1568, V, p. 439); Ludovico Guicciardini (already referred to); and Dominicus Lampsonius, *Pictorum aliquot celebrium Germaniae inferioris Effigies,* Antwerp 1572, n. 3; as well as Agorte da Molina,

Libro della Monteria que mandò escribior Don Alonso rey de Castilla, Seville 1582. But the most perceptive criticism, and indubitably the most in tune with modern taste, is that of J. de Sigüença, *Historia de la Ordén de San Geronimo,* III, *Descriptión del Monasterio de San Lorenzo del Escorial,* Madrid 1605, pp. 837-841. Bosch's reputation must have been enhanced considerably by the engravings of his friend, the architect Alaert du Hameel, now very rare indeed.

Bosch, however, had many imitators, but all fairly mediocre, and he lacked genuine disciples. However, Pieter Bruegel showed strong traces of his influence. Apart from the researches of Carel van Mander, who even in 1604 was lamenting that he knew nothing of Bosch's life (*Het Schilderboek,* Harlem 1604; translated into English by C. van De Wall, *Dutch and Flemish Painters,* New York 1936), and the catalogue of the works *quae supersunt* by J. B. Gramaye, *Taxandria,* Brussels 1610, we have to wait until the end of the last century to encounter a renewed critical interest in Bosch. A. Pinchart (*Archives des arts, sciences et lettres, Documents inédits,* I. Gand, 1860, pp. 267-78) begins the series of studies of the records of the Brotherhood, carried out systematically by J. Mosmans (*Jheronimus Anthoniszoon van Aken, alias Hieronymus Bosch. Zijn leven en zijn werk,* 's Hertogenbosch 1947), and by others. But the most important work, on which a large part of modern criticism depends, directly or indirectly, is that of Paul Lafond: *Hieronymus Bosch, son art, son influence, ses disciples,* Brussels 1914. Today, there a great number of monographs and studies of particular aspects of his work, as well as interpretations of his pictorial and demonic world. Interest in him has been increased by studies of demonology and the fantastic, by research into the passing of the Middle Ages, and also – indirectly – by psychological and psychoanalytical approaches. Here I will confine myself to giving a brief bibliography, summarizing the main trends, to provide a sample of modern critical attitudes. Ch. de Tolnay, *Hieronymus Bosch,* Basle 1937 (a key study, for the wide range of fields for research which it reveals and develops); J. Combe, *Jérôme Bosch,* 2nd ed., Paris 1957 (which emphasizes the alchemical sources of the painter's work); W. Fraenger, *Die Hochzeit zu Kana. Ein Dokument semitischer Gnosis bei Hieronymus Bosch,* Berlin 1950; *Der Tisch der Weisheit, bisher Die sieben Todsünden genannt,* Psyche, Stuttgart 1951; *The Millennium of Hieronymus Bosch: Outlines of a New Interpretation,* London 1952; Gillo Dorfies, *Bosch,* Milan 1954; W. Hirsch, ' Hieronymus Bosch and the Thinking of the Late Middle Ages ', *Konsthistorisk Tidskrift,* Stockholm 1957; A. Wertheim-Aymés, *Hieronymus Bosch, eine Einführung in seine geheime Symbolik,* Amsterdam 1957; R. Delevoy, *Bosch,* Geneva 1960. For works dealing with particular facets of Bosch's thought and symbolism, see: J. Baltrushaitis, *Le Moyen Age fantastique,* Paris 1960, already a classic; the study by E. Castelli, *Il demoniaco nell'arte: Il significato filosofico del demoniaco nell'arte,* Milan 1952; and that by Claude Roy, *Arts fantastiques,* Paris 1960.

Notes on the Text

[1] Here I wish to differ from the traditional identification of the Magi, followed by various authors on the basis of the work of Johannes von Hildesheim, which, though it goes back to the decade 1364-74, was widely known in Bosch's time.

[2] *Cf.* Mircea Eliade, *Méphistophélès et l'Androgyne,* Paris 1962; Part I, ' Expériences de la lumière mystique ', pp. 17-94. In the evidence which Eliade has collected, the experience which most closely resembles that of Bosch is recorded by Warner Allen in his book *The Timeless Moment,* London 1946, pp. 30, 33.

[3] Cf. Maurice Aniane, ' Note sur l'alchimie, " Yoga " cosmologique de la chrétienté médiévale ', in *Yoga, Science de l'homme intégrale,* Les Cahiers du Sud, Paris 1953, pp. 242-73.

[4] It is worth noting that the symbolic tradition of the broken egg, mentioned earlier, may be of Orphic derivation, as seen through tne alchemical interpretations of Zosimo.

[5] E. g., the twins from Rhain, in Bavaria, in an illustration by Bront, 1499. Cf. J. Baltrushaitis, *Réveils et prodiges: le gothique fantasque,* Paris 1960. p. 319.

[6] For the Renaissance doctrine of the three stages, see M. Eliade, ' Metallurgy, Magic, and Alchemy ', in *Zalmoxis, I,* 1938, pp. 85 ff. and idem, *Méphistophélès et l'Androgyne,* Paris 1962, especially pp. 122 ff. and p. 142.

Notes on the Plates

1-8 The Seven Deadly Sins. Madrid, Prado. 120 × 150 cm. This
painting, with a deep cleft in the centre, can be dated around 1475.
It forms part of the group of works which Philip II ordered to
be sent to the Escorial in 1574. But we know that this painting was
kept by him as a guide and warning in his own bedroom. Here
are depicted, in order: Sloth, Anger, Avarice, Gluttony, Envy, Pride,
and Lust. In the corners are the Four Last Things. In the centre,
the resurrected Christ, with the inscription: CAVE, CAVE, DEUS VIDET.
Above and below are two scrolls. This painting, which some consider
to be an *Imago mundi*, takes up the motif of the circle inscribed in a
square, common to the mystical tradition of various religions. It is
very similar to the Buddhist *mandala*, since it is designed, scene by
scene, to draw nearer to the Truth (Christ in the centre). And, like
the *mandala*, it is a mental image of the world – or rather a symbolic
projection both of the world and of the human spirit. Bosch's pessimistic world-view is already clearly evident.

9-10 The Cure of Folly. Oil on wood. 48 × 35 cm. Madrid,
Prado. A painting with a central *tondo* and an inscription in fine
Gothic script above and below. Can be dated between 1475 and
1480. Alludes, as do other works, to Dutch proverbs and sayings,
occasionally tranformed into poetic themes. A good bibliography
relevant here has been compiled by Robert L. Delevoy, *Bosch,* Geneva
1960, p. 131-2, which also refers to H. Meige, ' L'opération des
pierres dans la tête ' in *Aesculape*, XXIII, 1932, pp. 50-62. Stylistically the *tondo* is characterized by a breathtaking sense of immense
space in the landscape. It has been suggested that the city on 'the
horizon may be Nijmegen.

11 The Ship of Fools. Oil on panel, 32 × 56 cm. Paris, Louvre.
Some authorities have dated this between 1480 and 1490, but it
is plausible, to suppose that it was painted later than 1494, the
year in which the satirical poem of Sebastian Brant, *Das Narrenschiff*,
was published, and immediately translated into French and Latin;
or it might link up directly with the publication of Erasmus's *In
Praise of Folly*. There is, however, no need to seek its origins so late
in time, for the theme of the Ship of Fools can be found in the
moralistic writings of the fourteenth century. If certain stylistic
indications are taken into account, it is possible that the dating
originally proposed may be correct. The uncertainty is perpetuated
by the difficulty of defining Bosch's stylistic development, for lack
of dates.

12-23 The Hay-wain. Oil on panel. Central panel 135 × 100 cm.;
wings, 15 × 45 cm. Madrid, Prado. This triptych was painted between
1480 and 1485. Signed. It is the first of the great triptychs; a copy

of it exists in the Escorial. It is based on the Dutch proverbs about hay – all alluding to greed and fraud: 'The world is a heap of hay; everyone grabs some while he may.' The painting was acquired by Philip II and kept at the Escorial before being transferred to the Prado. On the closed wings of the triptych, there is a first version of the *Prodigal Son* (*The Vagabond*) of Rotterdam – possibly representing the man who succeeds in escaping from the folly of the world.

24-33 The Adoration of the Magi (or The Epiphany). Oil on wood. A signed painting that is, in some ways, Bosch's masterpiece. Given by the Bronckhorst and Bosshuyse families to the Chapel of the Brotherhood of Our Lady in the cathedral of 's Hertogenbosch, it escaped a first wave of iconoclastic frenzy on 22 August 1566. Moved to the Town Hall, it was then taken to Brussels, to the house of Jean de Casembroot, lord of Backerzeele. It was confiscated by Philip II on 14 April 1567, and transferred to the Escorial in 1574 (cf. A. Pinchart, *Archives des Arts, Sciences, et Lettres, Documents inédits*, Ghent 1860, I, p. 276). Later than the *Epiphany* now in Philadelphia, it appears to be linked in date with the *Temptation of St Anthony* in Lisbon (to judge from the similitarities in colouring). On the back is the *Mass of St Gregory*, in monochrome.

34 The Marriage at Cana. Oil on panel. 93 × 72 cm. (detail). Rotterdam, Boymans-Van Beuningen Museum. The painting is inspired by the Gospel story, but also by the passage from the Epistle of St Paul to the Corinthians (x. 20, 21): 'But I say that the things which the Gentiles sacrifice, they sacrifice to devils, and not to God: and I would not that ye should have fellowship with devils. Ye cannot drink the cup of the Lord and the cup of devils: ye cannot be partakers of the Lord's table, and of the table of devils...'. The composition may be connected – though rather speculatively – with the 'swan feast', organized by the Brotherhood in 1488, but it probably dates from rather later. It may be observed that the face of the husband is similar to that of St John the Evangelist on Patmos; and this – on comparison of the two paintings – inclines one to favour a later date. On this painting, see W. Fraenger, *Die Hochzeit zu Kana, Ein Dokument semitischer Gnosis bei Hieronimus Bosch*, Berlin 1950.

35-7 The Last Judgment. Oil on wood. Triptych, central panel 164 × 127 cm.: side panels 164 × 60 cm. Vienna, Akademie der bildenden Künste. Triptych. According to R. L. Delevoy (*Bosch*, Geneva 1960, pp. 109-10), this might be a copy of a lost painting, and could probably be attributed to the best of Bosch's pupils, Peter Huys. But it is likely that the triptych is authentic (though other writers – for instance Combe in the *Enc. Univ. dell'Arte* – do not recognize it), for it seems to be directly inspired, at least in part, by hallucinations produced by drugs. It is undoubtedly connected with the apocalyptic and symbolic content of Tondalus's *Vision*. It comes from the collections of the Archduke Leopold Wilhelm.

38-9 Paradise and the Ascent to the Empyrean. Oil on panel. 56.5 × 39.5 cm. Venice, Palazzo Ducale. Wooden panels, perhaps part of a ' Last Judgment '. While the ' Ascent to the Empyrean ' probably derives from a phrase of Ruysbroek's, who in his *Ornamento delle Nozze Spirituali*, speaks of the ' radiance ' of God, considering it as an ' abyss ' formed by a huge nucleus of light, the ' Paradise ' is – as Jacques Combe points out (' Bosch ', *Encic. Univ. dell'Arte*, II, cols. 746 and 747) – much more conventional, and has an entirely different concept of space, comparable to that of the *Temptations of St Anthony* at Lisbon. In actual fact, the symbolic and spatial conception of the ' Ascent ' is unique in the extant works of Bosch. His success in Venice is verified by the fact that Marcantonio Michiel, in 1521, saw a number of Bosch's works in Cardinal Grimani's house.

40 Last Judgment. Brussels, Musée communal. A version of the *Last Judgment* in Vienna, in which a great many of Bosch's favourite symbols recur, and in which there is a preponderance, which cannot be fortuitous, of objects made of metal.

41 Christ Mocked. Oil on wood, 73.7 × 59 cm. London, National Gallery. A painting acquired by the Gallery at the Hollingwood-Magniac sale. Two other similar subjects: one at Antwerp, the other in the Prado. In all these paintings the figure at the top, on the right, is based on the same model.

42-43 Christ Mocked (Ecce Homo). Madrid, Escorial. Comes from the collection of Philip II. Possibly shows the influence of Van der Weyden. It may be observed that the face of the executioner is the same as in the *Christ Mocked* in London, and recurs in a copy at Antwerp. It may perhaps be a little earlier than the *Ascent to Calvary* at Ghent (*pls* 46-47).

44 Ecce Homo. Oil on panel, 75 × 61 cm. (detail). Frankfurt, Stadelsches Kunstinstitut (a version is in Boston, Museum of Fine Arts). Signed. With this work may be linked the *Ecce Homo* in Philadelphia, also signed. The *Ecce Homo* exemplifies a particular kind of scenery and design which are probably connected with the artist's knowledge of, and experience in, theatrical design; it shows, too, the kind of expressive and structural mastery that Bosch displays in his finest works. This belongs to the painter's earliest phase.

45 Ascent to Calvary. Oil on panel, 52 × 32 cm. (detail). Vienna, Kunsthistorisches Museum. The authenticity of this has been disputed, but it is certainly by Bosch. (*Cf.* also R. L. Delevoy, *Bosch*, Geneva 1960, p. 125.) Probably dates from a period before his full maturity.

48-49 The Temptation of St Anthony. Oil on wood, 70 × 51 cm. Madrid, Prado. This is one of Bosch's best works. Probably dates from shortly before his death, possibly from 1515. From the hagiographic point of view, it is a genuinely unique work, and is isolated in the compass of the painter's stylistic evolution.

The Temptation of St Anthony (*ill. on p. 23*). Oil on wood, central panel 131.5 × 119 cm. Lisbon, Museo Nacional.

50-1 The Temptation of St Anthony. Madrid, Prado. Belongs to the same period as the *St John the Baptist in the Wilderness*. Dates, probably, from around 1505. From the hagiographic and stylistic point of view, this is less unusual and isolated than the preceding painting, but equally loaded with significance.

52-3 St Jerome at Prayer. Oil on wood. 77 × 59 cm. Ghent, Musée des Beaux-Arts, probably later than 1505. The saint pinioned to the crucifix himself dispels the symbols of heresy which surround him. According to J. Combe, the painting might have been inspired by an idea of Ruysbroeck's, expressed in his *Dat boec van den gheesteleken Tabernacule*, where the attitude is one of rejection of the duplicity and inconstancy of the world.

54-5 Altarpiece of the Hermits. Oil on wood. Central panel, 86.5 × 86.0 cm.; side panels, 86.5 × 29 cm. Venice, Palazzo Ducale. As a whole, the painting represents – with St Anthony (left) St Giles (right) and St Jerome (centre) – the three stages of the mystical elevation of the soul, according to the doctrines of Ruysbroeck. Stylistically linked with the *St Anthony* in Lisbon, and the *Garden of Earthly Delights,* the triptych is full of new symbols, especially in the central panel.

56 St John the Baptist in the Wilderness. Oil on wood, 48×40 cm. Madrid, Museo Lazaro-Galdiano. Perhaps originally formed part of a triptych which was later taken apart and divided transversely. It is among Bosch's most expressive and clearcut paintings – from the compositional point of view also.

57 Fragment of a 'Last Judgment'. Oil on panel, 60 × 114 cm (detail). Munich, Alte Pinakotek. According to Charles de Tolnay, this is a fragment of a *Last Judgment* commissioned in 1504 by Philip the Handsome. Here the demonic themes take on a decorative value. According to R. Delevoy, it dates from 1504.

58-9 St Julia Altarpiece. Oil on panel. Central panel, 104 × 63 cm., side panels each 104 × 28 cm. Venice, Palazzo Ducale. Signed triptych. In the centre, the martyrdom of the saint. In the right-hand panel, a monk and an armed man in a fantastic passage; in the left-hand one, the temptation of St Anthony. Difficult to date, because of the stylistic diversity of the panels. Possibly earlier than 1505.

60-79 The Garden of Earthly Delights. Oil on wood. Overall size, 195 × 202 cm. A triptych belonging to the artist's last period, despite the divergent view of Tolnay, who would place it around 1500-5, following the traditional chronology of Baldass. The writing on the outside, on the Creation of the World, runs: IPSE DIXIT ET FACTA SUNT, IPSE MANDAVIT ET CREATA SUNT.

Accidia

Auaricia

gula

Invidia

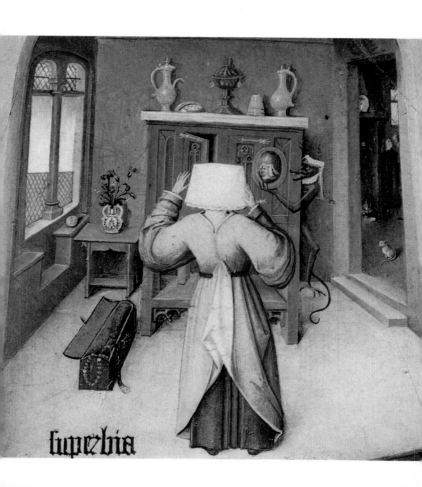

Superbia

luxuria

Ihcronimus bofch

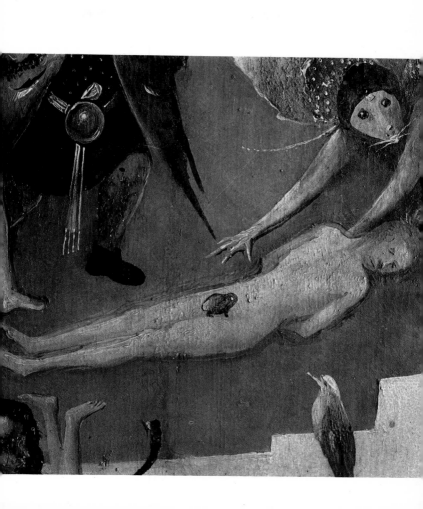

31

45

Iheronimus Bosch

55

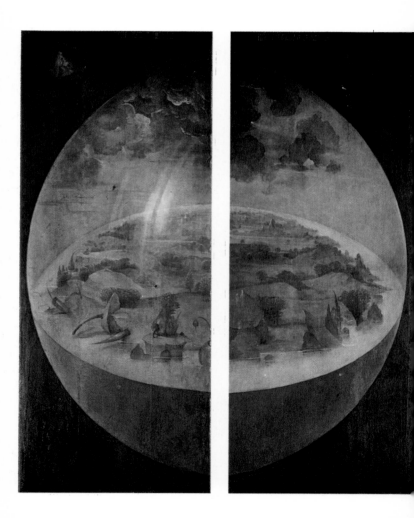

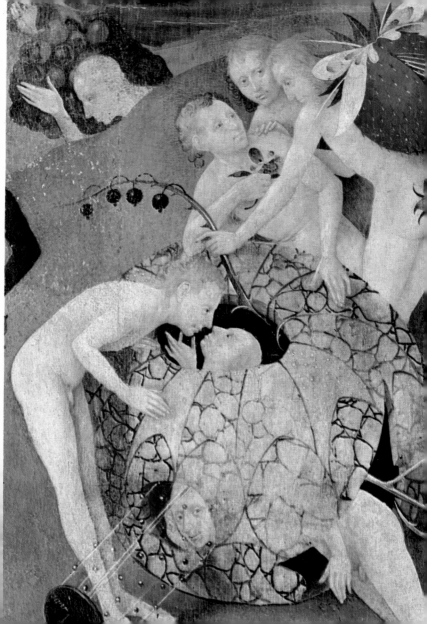